If My Tongue Refuses to Remain in My Mouth

Bloomington, Indiana *ÆB*

If My Tongue Refuses to Remain in My Mouth

By Sunwoo Kim

Translated by Won-Chung Kim
& Christopher Merrill

This is an Autumn Hill Books book
Published by Autumn Hill Books, Inc.
1138 E. Benson Court
Bloomington, IN 47401 USA

Copyright © 2018 by Autumn Hill Books
English translation © 2018 by Won-Chung Kim and Christopher Merrill
All rights reserved. Published in 2018.

First published in 2000 by Changbi Publishers as
내 혀가 입 속에 갇혀 있길 거부한다면
© 2000 under Kim Sun-Woo

The publication of this book was generously supported by the Korean Literature
Translation Institute

Design and layout by Justin Angeles
Cover image from a painting by Jong-ki Chae

ISBN 9780998740010
Library of Congress Control Number: 2018933089

A̸B

part two

part three

introduction

Sunwoo Kim's debut collection of poems, *If My Tongue Refuses to Remain in My Mouth*, appeared in 2000, declaring in the boldest terms that at the outset of the new millennium she would bring to the page a radically different conception of poetry. Central to her work is the belief that in what Lao Tzu calls "the world of ten thousand things" the poet reveals the manifold ways in which one thing is connected to another, her poetic self expanding into the world even as the world flows into her. This interconnectedness marks a return to a maternal, communal, and ecological view of the human condition. All is fluid in her poems, whether in verse or prose, surging and ebbing, swirling and flowing, and all is subject to the inscrutable measures of the universe, which she duplicates in lines that are by turns playful and profound: "In the body of the Buddha, who preached no difference between the visible and the invisible, the stonemason carved his desire—his agony!"

For Sunwoo Kim is a cartographer of desire: "I would rather be abandoned after loving fiercely," she writes, "than suffer from never loving anybody." The evidence suggests that she loves with all her heart, since the current of desire running through her work is by turns intimate, exuberant, inconsolable, revelatory, and memorable. In "Radish Flowers," for example, she enters her house "after a long absence" and feels something strange: "Someone had been there." A search of the closet and sink reveals nothing, and then she sees that buds have sprouted from a bit of radish saved to put in a bowl. "You must have made love!" she exclaims. "The air that couldn't pass you by / stayed with you." This is the air we breathe, nourishing, healing, and sustaining us, like Sunwoo Kim's poems, which offer life lessons in the boundless work of love.

Born in 1970 in Kangneung, Sunwoo Kim studied Korean literature in college and lives now in Chuncheon, in Kangwon Province, where she is a full-time writer. After the publication of her third volume of poems, *Who Is Sleeping in My Body?*, she brought out the first of her four novels, *I Am a Dance*, as well as several books of nonfiction, including *When the Moon Opens Underwater*; her fifth collection of poems, *A Nocturne*, appeared in 2016. For her work she has received the Modern Literary Award, the Hyundae Literary Award, and the Cheon Sang-Byung Poetry Award. An ardent environmentalist, she has participated in demonstrations against the construction of a naval base on Jeju Island and dams on Korea's four major rivers: direct actions that inform her poems, which are thick with images of the natural world.

Water, especially, which flows and pools and scatters in the pages of *If My Tongue Refuses to Remain in My Mouth*: "Ah, the sound of water," she notes, "is the very sound that comes from my body." Lotus flowers are always on the verge of opening in her work, according to the poet Heeduk Ra, tearing the flesh of the water. From the warm amniotic sea to the rapids of a stream Sunwoo Kim is ever on the alert for the liquid ways in which a life may unfold. "The night was coming when red spots of fever would break out on the birch tree, bare as the moon," she writes, "and pour down petals, bloody discharges, the last petals like river water." Indeed the law of circularity and return, the Buddhist concept that each thing is in constant circulation, changing from one state of being to another before eventually returning to its original state in order to recommence the journey of transmigration, guides her navigation of the world. As she writes in a poem for her sister, "That Reeking Tree at Seonun Temple":

With a knapsack on your back, you entered the platform,
saying, "Let's decompose ourselves.
If only we could squeeze a drop of clear water out of our rotting bodies!"

A wooden drum rings.
In the salty, fermented sound of the drum,
the reeking tree at Seonun Temple, fermenting
water from everywhere, assails me.

A word about the translation: this is the seventh book of poems on which Professor Won-Chung Kim and I have collaborated, and in each case we have followed the same working method. He provides me with an English trot (I have no Korean), which I gingerly pick my way through, at once mindful of my linguistic shortcomings and hopeful that my guesswork will bear fruit. Won-Chung's superb English — he completed his doctorate in English literature at the University of Iowa — and lifelong study of contemporary American poetry, which he teaches at Sungkyunkwan University in Seoul, make my task all the pleasanter; whenever I stray too far from the original, he reels me in, and as we go back and forth via email, trading successive drafts until the book is complete, a rhythm takes hold, which begins to govern the shape of the work. The virtue of a long collaboration is that each partner learns to anticipate the other's customary moves, which must be resisted in order to find the truest meaning, and the best English version, of a phrase or line, and in this way the book acquires a certain light, which from my vantage point allows me to understand something vital about a land half a world away — and in the depths of my soul.

— *Christopher Merrill*

The Old Pass at Daekwan-ryeong

At the beginning of January, I climb
the old pass at Daekwan-ryeong, under a blizzard watch.
Through memory's fault lines ice flowers shoot up
in many shapes and colors.

I cut a bundle of flowers from the boughs of a pine
and stuff them in my mouth — firewater.

Pungent steam rises
and my breath stops, like boiled alveoli. Slowly,
my throat warms, and the tears stored in my stomach,
gall bladder, and intestines rise up in an instant.
To get really hot is
to arrive at the freezing point.
The frozen red fruit of the dogwood
drops on my instep, *thud*.

When I go crazy missing something
and doubt seizes me — have I loved well enough? —
I walk alone toward the ice flower-covered old pass at Daekwan-ryeong
which no one likes to climb.

Brushing my lips against the hot trunk of the winter birch
as if for the first time,
I whisper, "Will you come, too?"

Eorayeon

I hear the sound of my mother washing herself
in the depths of the Eorayeon valley
in Jeongseon, Kangwon Province.

"My body often turns colors shamefully
as if I was twenty years old,"
she says, scraping autumn leaves from her breasts.

Red dots here and there in the blue water of Eorayeon.
"Leave them alone, Mom, they're beautiful."

The water in Eorayeon is deep;
I could not go to Eorayeon,
where the bier of cloud flowers flows.

On the Toilet

When I was young, I used to follow my mother to the field of green onions and empty my bowels on the embankment. She would wipe my bottom with soft pumpkin leaves. I wonder if I was ashamed when the thistle flowers swayed beautifully beside the dung heap, or if a slight stink reeked from her head towel when my soft warm dung cooled, little by little, in the midday sun. "Hey, stand guard for me!" Mom's hips, glimpsed under the pumpkin tendrils, would soften my mood. I wonder if I was elated when she said, "The dung of your children is fertilizer," and threw my dried dung onto the heap.

Seated on the toilet in the evening, I think of my steaming heap of dung. What I ate today will fertilize nothing.

Bee Nirvana

As if it had traveled through a long winding tunnel,
the bee fell into the pot containing a weeping fig
by the small window in my room.
Its parted wings grasped the empty sky,
and the atmosphere began to bustle.

("Honey, the pomegranate flowers are open...." Mother was hanging laundry.)

While I smoked a cigarette, leisurely,
the sky was seized and freed over a hundred times.
Painful, yes, and it occurred to me
that now it was time to end it all.
With my ring finger I dug a grave under the weeping fig
and buried the bee; white clouds
quietly passed and gathered a thousand times.

("Honey, the pomegranate flowers are falling...." Mother was sweeping the yard.)

No, perhaps it wasn't pain!
For the first time in its life,
under the weeping fig, by the small window in my room,
the bee seemed to meet pollen
from centuries ago, which scattered in the sunlight or the air,
and enjoy the heavy breathing of sexual communion.
I let spill a handful of dust grabbed furtively.

("Honey, look at these pomegranates. They look like your gums when you were born.")

My Mother's Bones and Three Does* of Sweet Rice

That woman is dead.
The liver spots are vividly alive on the face of the dead woman.
The dead woman becomes a garden for white flower shaman mushrooms.†

The dead woman's sealed
genitals and breasts open wide.
Like the powder of the white cabbage butterfly,
fine white dust — sparkling eggs — scatters in the wind.

After death, I will not be buried in your family grave mound.
She asks me to cremate her body, to finely grind three *does* of sweet rice,
and then to mix her bone waste with sweet rice powder
to scatter on a windy day, on the broad flat rock of Siroo Mountain.

If it's mixed with sweet rice powder,
wild animals and birds will not avoid it but eat as they please,
the rest will be carried off by the wind,
lightly, to every corner of the earth.
Three *does* of sweet rice! How long
has she harbored this queer desire?

That woman, laying delicate white eggs,
tosses and turns her rustling body,
which is becoming a garden for white flower shaman mushrooms.
Like every mother who loses three *mals* of blood in childbirth,
my mother keeps a shroud and three *does* of sweet rice
in her closet, and waits for it.
Actually, she has always been waiting for it.

*Doe is a traditional Korean unit of measure, about 1.8 liters (Translators' note).
†Botanical name: *Russula alboaxeolata* (Translators' note).
·Mal is a traditional Korean unit of measure. 1 *mal* equals 10 *does*, about 18 liters
(Translators' note).

Mokpo Port

There is time to return,
not because of the desolation of the port after the last ship has departed,
but because of the peaches of the old woman crouching in the waiting room.

There is time for my wound to become infected,
while I pick out the healthy flesh
of the peaches, feeling sorry for the bruised and festering one.

Fruits that travelled so far to arrive here!
Is it because visible wounds are not the only ones
that the inner yard of my still-green life smells so fishy?

With my finger I search for my heart.
Scales of flesh sometimes fall from me like dry leaves.
Did I hear the whistle? Did I love?
Like a straw effigy with dozens of needles in its heart,
which does not know its wounds are wounds,
I leave and return to Mokpo port, swinging my arms
without experiencing the relief of spilling blood, not even a single drop.
I would rather be abandoned after loving fiercely
than suffer from never loving anybody.

The last departed ship enters my body.

Her Salt Ponds

Last night, when the first snowflakes fell, I saw the laundry woman crying. She often cries under the clothes hanging from the eaves, or in front of the rabbit hutch at the pet shop next door.

When she cries under clothes that might have covered other bodies, she only cries a little. And as she cries she takes them down with a long stick and shakes them. The clothes swing perilously, and soon her tears stop.

Crouching before the rabbit hutch, she cries for a while, holding a red plastic dipper, brushing her teeth for a long time, crying until the red-eyed rabbit turns its face away.

The next morning I pass her salt ponds in silence. She folds her left hand like a stake over her right, which grips the iron handle. Lifting her shoulder, she puts all her energy into the ironing board.

Two blank black salt ponds gaze at her praying hands. Nor will she turn the water-wheel for a while.

Who Else Besides Us Lay in this Rice Bowl?

This house
is a rice bowl of rats,
of cockroaches,
of the long dead
who lay down as if in a coffin,
of memory,
of suffering bedsores,
of a sickly peach tree
that oozes hot, salty, sticky tears.
A rice bowl of bruised clouds,
of wounds.
Lest this rice bowl of a house

be empty and hungry,
you and I lie down in the bowl.
You have the best smell in the world,
the smell of steamed rice filled with tears.

*Dharma** in the Beehive*

I visited the Sudo hermit of Bulyeong Mountain,
had a bout with the Vairocana Buddha*.

When I teased him, asking, Why are Buddhas of the Silla Dynasty
so sexy? he slowly raised his half-closed eyelids.
When I tickled his waist, saying the pronunciation of Silla
sounds romantic, he waved his hand. Damn you, he said.
I said, Princess Seonhwa and Seodong† wouldn't care
about the symmetrical beauty of thousand-year-old art works.
Don't you envy the heated glances of Asdal and Asanyeo'?
Ha, he laughed. The pretty ear lobes
of the Vairocana Buddha turned red.

In the body of the Buddha, who preached no difference between the visible and
    the invisible,
the stonemason carved his desire — his agony!

A beehive as big as a fist hangs under the cracked body
of the three-storied stone pagoda standing peacefully before the Buddhist sanctuary.
Stone flowers blossom and fall for a thousand years,
the evanescent dharmas come in and out of the beehive, and the skirts of
handsome men and women brush endlessly.

Whoops! What's this?
I violated the Buddha, and here I am.

*Often called the primordial or supreme Buddha, representing the wisdom of *sunyata*, or "emptiness" (Translators' note).

†Seodong (later King Moo of Baekje) fell in love with Soenhwa, princess of Silla, wrote and spread a scandalous song about her, and finally succeeded in marrying her (Translators' note).

˙Asadal, a master stonemason, built the Seokga Pagoda (National Treasure 21). His wife, Asanyeo, could not bear his long absence during its construction and committed suicide (Translators' note).

Suicide of the Mother Tree 1

When my grandmother passed it, she would clasp her hands in prayer. When I had pneumonia as a child, she would take me there. Please cure my granddaughter with clean water and breath. Then the tree would raise the salt wind with a soughing sound to touch the nape of my neck.

Under the old gingko tree, where yellow leaves rain, my grandmother was relieving herself. When I rushed to her in joy, she changed into my mother. What a strange dream! Gingko leaves sparkling with drops of urine were flying upward onto Daekwan-ryeong ridge.

They said she died; she had a long illness and then was struck by lightning. A man said emphatically that a new road would be paved on that ground; the price of the lot would rise.

Strange that the word *suicide* occurs to me: road of no dreams. Her despair for humanity, her will to die—maybe they invited the thunder. Broken boughs, bleeding mothers walking out of the fruits hanging from the tree.

My daydream of climbing over Daekwan-ryeong resembled my mother's premonition of my conception. I could see that distant afternoon when the gingko tree—limping in through a gap of warm sky—took a walk in her body. I could see the newborn baby me disappearing with a glitter into the wrinkles of the atmosphere, which has turned old in the blink of an eye.

Radish Flowers

In this house
lies something as big as the house.

When I opened the door after a long absence
something felt strange: someone had been here.
But when I opened the closet and looked into the sink:
nothing different. My mind sank,
I flopped onto my bed. Catching my breath, I saw

radish flowers.
Buds had sprouted like deer horns
from the bit of radish I had saved to put in a bowl.

You must have made love!
The air that couldn't pass you by
stayed with you.
Contained in the corner of the empty house,
the radish flowers fight
the wound.

The Neck of the Rapids

I didn't know until I came to the Mureung rapids
that water has bones.

Feeling sorry for the hearts of scooped-up stones embracing moss-covered
   stones,
and the hearts of large stones crossing over small ones,
water secretly bends its body,
its drops bouncing.

The foreheads of stones redden, water folds—
one fold added onto another.
Ah, the sound of water
is the very sound that comes from my body.

To lean toward you
I even had to bend my bones.

Whistle Stop

In memory, my still-green love
is the boy I saw the day the persimmon flowers fell.
We dug up the covering of fine dust
by the zinc-roofed houses, as if to cast a spell.
"I-Like-You" appeared like eyelashes.
"Na-na-na, boo-boo," his friends teased,
and so with his head bowed he wrote in the dust,
"I'm sorry."
A boy from Dangdoo village
with the scent of dried pine boughs.

I never saw him again after I moved
and came to know men.
Visiting my hometown, I heard
he had moved to Taebaek with his father,
dropped out of technical school, became a miner.
I often thought about that whistle stop,
where express trains never stop.
Warming its hands with a bowl of noodles
in the depots of Sabook, Cheolam, and Hwangji,
the local train slowly approaches the East Sea.

He's the whistle stop of my memory.
They say he works as an ironsmith in Garibong
and has a boy, still unregistered.
Maybe he writes under a wall—
life, wielding rod, spark, hope,
words he didn't know when he was young.
I often think of that father of a child—
the boy from Dangdoo village with the scent of dried pine boughs:
the pungent smoke constricts my vocal cords.

That Reeking Tree at Seonun Temple
for Yeondeok Monk, my sister in her 40s

I came to Seonun Temple
and sat under the gingko tree by the outhouse.
Because of the foul smell, I checked my backside,
and found ripe gingko nuts.

It was the smell of baby poop: rather sweet.
If only we could open our lower bellies like that
and grow nuts that look like the first feces of a newborn!

I was reminded of you.
What was at the top of the stairs
when in your claustrophobia you rushed up
from the Seoul subway station, shouting "Phaa?"

With a knapsack on your back, you entered the platform,
saying, "Let's decompose ourselves.
If only we could squeeze a drop of clear water out of our rotting bodies!"

A wooden drum rings.
In the salty, fermented sound of the drum
the reeking tree at Seonun Temple, fermenting
waste water from all time, assails me.

I Walk into the Water of an Autumn Cloud

In my mother's room, in the house of my childhood,
my mother and I took a nap one afternoon.
A sea swell rolled over her belly.
The antique cabinet inlaid with mother-of-pearl,
which she had brought with her to her marriage, was as old and sick as her;
out of the body on which the mother-of-pearls cut
from a conch shell was covered over
cranes flew
and a turtle crawled in a cloud.
The moon climbing down the pine tree
splashed into the water, and when I opened the first page
of the book of somnambulism the pine and cranes
were stuck in a circle, in a womb of water.
The sound of water smeared the golden shell
of the conch, in which for so long
the sea had trimmed and folded page after page.
Many "I"s, spawned on waterweeds,
floated over the edge.
It was an autumn afternoon when my mother and I were soaked
in the cabinet inlaid with mother-of-pearl, which she had brought to her marriage.

part two

2

Dogtooth Violet

My old love called me at midnight
and asked if I ever masturbate.
I said I do sometimes.
He asked who I think about when I do it.
"No one," I said,
though I asked, "Does a flower open
its buds only when it thinks of butterflies and bees?"
He couldn't understand my words.
The dogtooth violet...
the flower raising a feeble stalk
through hard-packed soil and unmelted snow
on a hill below Namhaekeumsan came to mind.
The feel of sunlight on the stalk
and the old longing of moisture to tickle rootlets
at the start of the thaw made my breasts swell.
"In the language of flowers dogtooth violet means wanton woman.
Do you think the wind shakes the stalk?
It's the passion within the stalk that produces the wind.
See how its two legs lie down like grass."
Even with no one to knock it down,
a dogtooth violet is a dogtooth violet.
It burns hot as hardwood charcoal.

Graves Raise Babies

The leaves of the plane tree lay down in the street, facing westward, and at the end of the street the dove's body was left in the clear track of a car.

"Even a bird's intestines are heavy." My sad lover, who lingered long over the body, fluttered, hiding half of the pale leaf.

Did I whisper the words, hugging my love, as blood-smeared feathers floated endlessly up in my wine glass?

"Think of the insides of a newborn. A tiny garden in which red dahlias let off steam and cogon grass paves a pale green road. Red and white water drops and phytol cavort on yellow and orange rose moss and taro leaves. The drops are round graves. We're all the warm house of the grave."

Hanging from my breast like a seed leaf, my young love cried. Pain passed gently over my ripening areola, and I opened my breast-grave to offer my nipple.

I don't know how my love stopped crying that day.

He has become my five-year-old brother returning home on my back, after burying the dove on the outskirts of the village. "Thank you," he says. "Someday I'll be a mother to you." A smooth fragrance rises from his garden. Milk seems to be swelling in my breast-grave.

Onset of Spring

I want to have a baby.
For the seaweed-like little life
that begins to learn how to breathe,
I want to have a round belly
with whom to share my breath.

For the life that grows within my body
I want to share my rice and soup
and take a little rest,
talking
and sharing bodies when words fail.

In the noon-of-conception dream where I gather
and embrace within my skirt star lights
variegated in the well at the village entrance,
where white-skinned pebbles touch each other's bodies and grow,

the smell of celandine*
spreads over the far field.

*In Korea, celandine (*chelidonium majus*) is called the baby poo flower, since yellow fluid flows from its cut stem (Translators' note).

History

On her sixty-sixth birthday, when my mother was sick in bed,
I went home and saw it when I helped her urinate.
Her pubis must once have been a forest of brush
where the moon swelled with the overripe love
of grasshoppers on hot humid nights.
Now a steep dusty hill has taken its place.
The saying that the private parts of a woman
who spent her youth in a steep field
resemble that very field thunders and rains in my mind—
I'm soaked from cleaning my mother's body.
In the sparse foothills of her body
I find a lonely, desolate form of peace
in which fruits return to flowers, seeds, and soil.
Mother raises her knees in shame,
and her steep field,
having already completed preparations to return,
looks like the flat genitalia of a little girl.

The Night of Round Memory

The thought of a radish flower stalk pickled in soybean paste sails over my home-town garden when I cook mackerel soup with chopped radishes and scoop a bowl of water kimchi. Earthen pots nap under the ripe sun. "They're also breathing!" My sixty-year-old mother opens the window, embracing her memory of the last month of her pregnancy.

My mother with nine children chews Saridon* nine months a year. When I wash my shape-memory underwire bra, I feel a sudden pain down below. The memory of a round breast recovering its original shape even as you twist it up to dry. After the winter of the miscarriage, I wonder where the bird that flew quickly through my private parts lives before it returns in spring to nest.

A matting needle is tucked into her dress. Anxiously, I urge her to take it out, tear the mackerel flesh, and place it on her spoon. "You were a breech baby, and for two hours you searched for the way out. I thought your way did not exist in my body." O memory of roundness and warm amniotic fluid, I might have wished to stay there a little longer.

"I was mad for peaches when I carried you in my belly." I peel a peach and offer her the soft flesh. Her false teeth click. "It's getting dark. Cover the lids on the pots. It's time for dinner." To make dinner for my grandfather, who died eight years ago, she hurries outside. Her cloth collar ripples over Daekwan-ryeong Pass. It's because of memory that the peach grows round.

*A popular painkiller in Korea (Translators' note).

Wine Glass, the Word of the Wind

When her lips touched my breast
I perceived the trace.
My wound widened like a whistle,
and she walked into my world.

In the world before the glass, when the wind bore me
and moonlight stroked my brow, I was but a handful of sand.
At that time I could understand longing,
because it was my congenital sister. She came to me
as a woman whose heart had not been broken yet,
setting a wounded bee in the red petals of crape myrtle.
We danced for a long time in the moonlight.
The wind drew river water down her spine,
and we laid petals on the wound
because we were naked, we had nothing to wear,
having conceived a shard-shaped star from a handful of sand.

She prepared to leave before dawn.
The road had been erased,
neither moonlight nor petals could be seen.

She came back the next day, she didn't recognize me.
"Do you know what a fatal weakness hope is?"
She spat out a few curses, guzzled hard liquor,
fixed her makeup, and left.
The mark of her lips is clear on my breast,
the crape myrtle petals fell, opening a red ovary.

Sancheong Inn

On the last day of my trip, I was lying down, staring blankly at the white wall. As usual in old inns, I found graffiti like "I love you" and "I'm leaving tomorrow." There was a discolored purple stain in the corner where the walls met. I gazed at it with a strange excitement.

A woman emerged from the corner, the beginning and end of two worlds. She smelled like the bud of a Siberian gooseberry. The fragrance that a surprised green bud releases the moment it touches the air of another world. She let me rest my head on her and gazed at me for a long time. "I haven't seen my face in the eyes of someone else for a while," I said, burying my face in her armpit.

When she moved, her body emitted various smells: the odor of a Formica chest of drawers, the fragrance of a wild rose rising from a dead greenfinch. My brow was burning. The smell of dust in a summer shower, the smell of my mother's under-wear ....I trembled, as if every cell had its own heart.

Throw away the sad posture in which we seem to have entered each other but did not, in which we face each other but turn away .... The smell of dried straw that doesn't need to feign excitement, the smell of a crumbled earthen wall, the fra-grance of melilot in my grandmother's shroud and the agalloch scattered on the streets in May — even these she smeared in my bones.

After she returned to the corner where time and space mingle, I woke slowly, thinking it smelled of the seawater that I sensed leaving her womb.

A Room at the Port

On nights of menstrual cramps,
I'd like to lay my body down on the sizzling floor.
When I climb down from the bed
and bury my nose in the pillow that smells of conch,

I become young raw stuff
like a blue salmon,
and pull my knees up, and hunch my shoulders.
Grown round enough to embrace
a soft turtle egg with my breast,
I want to suck the breast of the wave or offer it my breast,

watch the sun rising in the port,
shake my white bum up and down,
paddle in the water, and build a sand castle.

Though I boast that I can enjoy a mild fever now and then,
my fishy-smelling flesh goes to port first
when my mind suffers a relapse.
Even Buddha, Lenin, and my barefoot mother, when they were ill,
would not leave the floor like this all day long.
Even if a feverish girl mixes her flesh fiercely with the wave,
no one will blame her for it.

Women in the Water

When I sit down on the bank of the reservoir
and gaze into the water for a long time,
it's loud with the sound of drum and gong, with shoulders dancing
as if at a festival.

When Princess Bari* shakes the bell to open the sluice gate,
Empress Myeongseong† can be seen baking a steamed rice cake.
A cloud comes down and spreads its mat,
and a white bird flies off along the line of Hwang Jeeni's* parted hair,
writing a prayer, and the wind blows.
Burning prayer papers for her young children,
Nanseolheon‡ suddenly raises her eyes to gaze at the persimmon tree.
A butterfly kite caught in the treetop flutters.
Hwang Jeeni drapes a long hood over Nanseolheon.
The women look at each other and let out belly laughs.
Empress Myeongseong lays out a red pomegranate.
Three women shell and eat the sour fruit,
grimacing and laughing: *hahaha*.
Tear sprays.
Women who wander the world alone
beat *Huimori*± time. Mad as the currant,
the sky in the glass has wandered for a thousand years,
and paper money scatters.

What underwater feast is underway?
I place rice wrapped in lettuce in my mother's mouth,
and the spring day by the reservoir deepens its lament.

*One of the most important gods in Korean shamanistic ritual, Princess Bari was
the seventh daughter of a king who abandoned her because he wanted a son; when
he fell prey to a fatal disease, she was the only one willing to travel to the under-
world in search of the elixir of life. She underwent many ordeals to secure the
drug with which she brought her dead father back to life (Translators' note).
†Empress Myeongseong (1851-1895) was the first official wife of King Gojong,
the first emperor of the Korean Empire. She was assassinated by Japanese agents
(Translators' note).
˙A famous gisaeng and poet of the mid Chosun period (Translators' note).
‡A poet, writer, and painter of the mid Chosun period, Nanseolheon Heo (1563-
1589) wrote some three hundred poems, which were also published in Chinese
and Japanese, earning her international acclaim (Translators' note).
±A traditional time signature in Korean music, with a fast tempo that calls to mind
a sweeping wind.

Spring Afternoon

Only old people sit together in Tapgol Park at three in the afternoon.
Entering the public toilet, I laugh *cle-cle*.
Two old women with rouged cheeks, like brides,
push their faces against the broken mirror,
laughing *cle-cle*, tidying each other's hair.
"That old codger tried to seduce me — disgusting."
The word "Dis-gus-ting" flies off her tongue
cheerfully in a high pitch.
They open a puff powder box with a frayed cover
and apply Coty powder.
Tapgol Park at three o'clock on a spring afternoon
sheds flower petals and dapples on milky glass.
Young as I am, I laugh *cle-cle* like a cunning fox.
Crouching with my pants dropped,
I listen to their murmuring for a long time.
I'd like to see my pretty mother flirting.

Twilight

While the gingko sheds its leaves, as if in premature ejaculation,
flutters its white bone,
and glides with its fin through the twilight,

an old man loiters under the theater billboard.
He raises his head and takes the actress's nipple softly in his mouth.
His tongue sweetens, the mother of his childhood carries
a water jar on her head and offers him a dipper of her milk.
Embarrassed, he puts the earrings of a painted lady on her earlobes.
Milk flows from the image of this flower, which shakes whenever she smiles.
Hiding petals, the new bride lets loose birds from the hem of her cotton skirt.
His face turns red, so he offers her power puff. Children
tumble out of her underwear to fly a kite made of birdsong.
The indigo kite gabbles and flies into the twilight. On the kite,
his mother with bare feet opens her blouse and calls him.

Softly riding on the fin of the leafless gingko tree,
the old man swims into a suburban theater.
The last leaf glows deep red at twilight.

The Cuckoo that Cries Behind Me

I was lying under the magnolia tree, which swayed like a cabbage butterfly mobile, and cuckoos cried. Did we make love then?

It was almost Christmas when I met him. Snow fell only on our insteps, and we borrowed each other's shoulders because our feet were heavy. I could see clear nail marks on the back of his pale hand whenever he lifted his glass. Sometimes dark blood flowed, reminding us that no flower is red for more than ten days. Picking up the petals drowned in the glass, we laughed until we cried.

Eli eli lama sabachthani?! Should the question mark come after the exclamation mark? His fingers trembled when he neatly laid down his chopsticks. The table shook, the glass tipped over, the wet flag was stained. Footsteps came clear. How can we talk about hope without appropriating despair? *Eli…. eli, eli……* That night I pleaded with him to be my lover.

All I could give him was a bowl of clean water. Twice he wept in front of me. On one occasion he wept behind me, making me think he had hiccupped like a cuckoo. Hey, I want to make love with you under the magnolia tree in spring. Please come to me before the petals, unable to bear the weight of a shadow, cover my forehead. A vivid stain like a burnt spot will remain on your heart.

When he calmed down enough to stop crying, blood stopped flowing from the nail marks. "Please leave now," I said, picking up the iron nails under the magnolia tree.

Hemoglobin, Alcohol, and Hair

(I was happy when my head split open:
an external wound is less dangerous than an internal one.)

When I slit my wrist breaking paving blocks, my hair burned.
The 1980s were a decade of piercing external wounds:
when we hung strips of our flesh on the barricades,
new flesh appeared after a night's sleep.
This is neither soaking molars in the bitter waters of memory
nor an expression designed to help the enemy.

The 1990s were a decade of depressing internal wounds:
when people fell and sprained their ankles,
they suffered bruises without spilling any blood.
The days of our body, composed of ten times as many cells
as the world's population, are peaceful when no blood is shed.

But my head split open yesterday.
On my way home I lay down in the street, dead-drunk.
My skull was okay, the bruise was small,
but my hair bled like the fall
and dyed my friend's skirt and jacket red.
She told me that I lay in the street and, laughing blandly, said,
"Ah, it's refreshing."

Red dahlias (do you remember?)
marched out of a dream in bundles.
I wrote a letter but crumpled it
— My body seems to have no desire to protect me.
I just sent you a telegram.
— A hidden wound makes me wither.
Seized by a sudden fear,
I cry, severing the necks of the dahlias.

A Dot

I'm gazing at a blue dot
on the left buttock of my love.
Long ago, when I was you,
the blue dot was under my left breast.
I remember wandering all day in a field of flowers,
struck by a sudden desire to eat meat
when my geology teacher put a dot on the blackboard and said it was our galaxy.
Keeping a world within you, you crossed this far exhausted,
and I walked into your blue dot.
After flying over the blank hour of the blue dot
to once again find another blue star
my heart rests on the permanent snow.
You, please come into me. It is because you and I
are holding out as grass seeds on the edge of the steep bluff of a blue star
that I get angry sometimes,
and now and then my ignited bones
try to flow out of my body with the sound of water
when you enter me, at once huge and like a mustard seed.

part three

3

A Flame in the Lotus Pip

The house was heated with briquettes.
It was in Sabook, in 1989, and I had just turned twenty.
Lying down in my room in a flophouse, I thought of the hard black
lotus seeds jutting from the plate of ice on the winter pond —
a clump of lotus seeds deposited for so long it turned
black as a briquette. I wondered what cold underground
had opened so many holes in the lotus pip.
Though Sabook was cold even in March,
and breathing holes in a lotus pip was as dangerous as firing blindly at a target,
a door appeared silently, in a strange sort of peace,
through which an old woman — the innkeeper — entered
to check the floor and then went back out.
The inn had no sign — she also sold ramen and soju —
and when she told me she was from Gwangju,
the word sounded as distant as Loulan*.
That night I recalled Loulan as the dark side of the moon
and dreamed of riding a camel
toward Loulan.
The camel's hoof prints left holes in the sand,
which soon filled with sand,
the desert was all road. Like flames, snowflakes struck
the cracked windowpane clickety-clack:
the sound of a bonfire burning on an ice pond.
Both Sabook and Gwangju were ice ponds.

A piece of lotus pip jutting from the plate of ice
was cold as ashes resting in a strange peace,
and the stone I threw slid over the ice
to the corner.
While the briquettes burned down, the old woman
changed into a girl lighting charcoal before I knew it.
The ice pond was as warm as the holes in the charred briquettes.
In 1989, I was twenty,
and the history of my anemia was passing along with it.
It was the night on which someone transfused blood
silently into the holes of the lotus pip.

*An ancient city in China (Translators' note).

A Relationship

(I have something to confess. It's about a worm
that grows inside the body of a snail and lays its eggs there.)
Don't be afraid. It doesn't exterminate the host indiscriminately,
like a cancer cell. Neither crawling nor copulating
is a problem for me. You'll look for food
diligently and I'll grow quickly.
(Isn't it wonderful to raise something in your body?)
In truth, now that I have grown up,
you're too small and dingy to host me for the rest of my life.
I'm fated to spend my last years
in the cozy intestines of a bird.
Painlessly, I'll invade the tender stalk of your eye
and your head will exhale luster without knowing why.
Now you may enjoy your final saunter
before the claw of an imposing bird comes from afar
to hook your shining back.
Imagine rolling over the fallen leaves without a grave
after crawling on your belly for your whole life.
A lonely death is terrible. I'll let you fly over the cloud.
Tasting your mixed warm gravy,
I'll sing the most beautiful dirge for you.
You'll like your new home even as it crushes you.
By then you may understand everything,
though the end is set. I leave you with no debts.
(Isn't it amazing? It's you who raised me!)

The Pond in the Village

There was a pond
either east or west of the village.

It was said that women came there to deliver babies of the water
during the full moon, when the white water lilies opened.
A prophet — half-man, half-beast — was said to practice bird divination.
They said the forbidden fruit was really fragrant,
but no one would tell a stranger
how to get to the pond.

Upon returning from the pond, I told the villagers
it was nothing but a deep blue marsh
thick with fir trees and blackberry bushes.
A man came up to choke me.
Another man opened a straw bag.
There were gloomy eyes wielding flashlights
when I was thrown into the pond.

In the dark water,
among the plants wandering like ghosts,
I saw countless straw bags
standing on their heads, waving silently,
including the ones I threw away
casting phosphorescent light on me as I sank.

Either east or west of my mind
is a deep blue pond.

If My Tongue Refuses to Remain in My Mouth

I am in the process of killing him.

Camellia, an eelworm that has sucked blood to the full, falls in drops. He's busy picking and eating wriggling red worms. I push the scalpel deeper, his chest finally opens, and camellias clutching their necks gush out. Bloodless skeletons follow clitter-clatter. A baby skeleton holding its mother's neck smiles sweetly. A crippled skeleton offers rotten remnant apples. They are completely rotten. He opens his eyes wide, pushes back into his bowels what spilled out . . . . Every day I figure out how to kill him. He has grown so fat his skin no longer fits, and every day he visits my room holding a piece of skin. Though I sew new flesh onto his skin (this is how I make my living now), his body rapidly grows huge. I don't know where he peels off and brings new skin, it always smells like fresh blood. . . . Tonight I will kill him. He wants my last inner skin. Singing a sweet lullaby, he will peel off the skin of my loins. Tomorrow he'll bring pink artificial skin and sew it onto my body by himself, singing a rhythmical work song. I'll get a bonus, maybe an armful of red camellias too . . . .

I killed him again. And no court in the world will convict me, because my servile tongue is confined in his mouth.

A Clear Day

Passing the municipal office, I saw a wardrobe
whose legs had collapsed and drawers were missing.

Someone must have cast a look of pity on it,
and maintaining balance
might have been a double abasement.

When metal bands rotted
and a handful of dust fell from the doors,
the wardrobe must have sung with a willing heart:
wood from Odae Mountain
returns to the sunlight of Odae Mountain, and the nails,
which were my body for a while, return to the darkness of a mineral vein.

Whatever betrayed the desire of gravity to fasten
everything to its center, which was my bone for a while, is beautiful.
The moment it soars and splits, breaking its legs,
is the moment when it finally fulfills its love,
when it can dream of a love for which it may be stoned.

On a clear day good for dying
I saw a bright, hot heart
on which was pasted the waste collection permit.

Mousetrap

Entering the back door of my rented apartment late at night,
I met a humpbacked gray rat.
Had I seen it before?
I don't know why, but it looked familiar, so I slowed down.

Through its glassy eyeballs
my father walked into the back yard of our house in my hometown
holding a mousetrap and briquette tongs,
saying, "This wicked rat, this wicked r-a-t!"
Since that day, crumbling dried flowers have released a musty smell
in the attic of my adolescence.

"Well, rats can't help
but gnaw randomly at anything,
for their teeth grow long as spears
and poke their own body,"
whispered my sister under the blanket, blocking her ears.
And I would dream
the red-hot briquette tongs
seared and pierced the skin of my soul.

A drunken man in the neighboring house
looked blankly at me pacing back and forth,
his body shriveling, and crawled into the mousetrap.

A Noble Dining Table

I was enjoying the different dishes made for my birthday dinner —
steamed rice, stir-fried glass noodles and vegetables, spicy chicken stew,
salted mackerel, seaweed soup — when it struck me
that I have been eating my mother for twenty-eight years.

Since I was sowed in this planet
and raised with water, air, and earth, like spinach, chicken, and mackerel,
aren't we congenital brothers and sisters?
The thought that I have been sleeping with my father . . .

The chicken I am eating now,
whose innards are composed of
the elements that constituted my grandfather,
is my sister, and in my blood our flesh is mixed . . . .

The table of incest through many generations:
I'd like to climb naked and lay myself
down on this unavoidable,
bottomless table

so that my mother can eat me.

Cockroaches of All Nations

Why don't you fly with your wings?
If you had known the world was the tip of a lightning rod
you might have soared.

Thud! I slapped the rolled-up newspaper down on the cockroach.

My feelers, which you might have encountered somewhere,
are crushed.
Spilling its guts
and desperately suspending the egg sack on its tail,
the roach rolls on.
Spoiling and turning every "house" into rot and chaos,
the "sack" rolls on.

The Age of No Sperm

The number of sperm is diminishing,
they say, *hee-hee*.
The beakers in the lab
and the heads of fetuses will be liberated.

They say that on average sperm has decreased by forty percent
in the last forty years, the last decade showing a 2.6 percent decrease per year.
I laugh, *hee-hee*. The house ledger of prostitutes
will become 2.6 percent more solid.

Be grateful that it is not original sin
but a side effect of chemicals
accumulating in our bodies. *Hee-hee*, you're not the only one who ate them.

A peaceful end may come as a surprise.
Old men of five oceans and six continents may gather to cut
the windpipe of the last sacrifice, as at a neighborhood meeting.
May a cloud of fertilized eggs descend soon
and may we hear the crying of a human baby once more!

Among the animals with lungs and a womb
only humans exploit and kill one other.
Therefore, accept this willingly: the door of heaven will open
and a rotten umbilical cord will descend to pierce your lower abdomen.

The age of no sperm:
the souls of unfertilized eggs
will dye winter sorghum stalks red;
only red sorghum flowers will bloom wild
next year, and in the years to come.

Grandmother's Yard

When I played the stone-striking game by the mud wall—
"Girl, leave the stones in their original places"—
Grandmother weeded the vegetable garden,
the yellow day lilies were beautiful.

If without thinking you pour out hot slops
microorganisms in the earth will die.
When she turned in the back alley, her parted white hair
ruffled beautifully in the early morning sunlight.

"Girl, if you crush an anthill, Mr. Kite will cry."
The hooves of a baby roe deer on the mountain will shrivel
before a basket of rain clouds or a streak of misty rain.
White bush clover flowers will fall.

On an evening when the overpass hangs obliquely
from the mud walls and storm windows of vanished memory,
the white socks of my grandmother, whose mind knows no rest,
wander blankly in the cold rain.

Empty House

The empty house
suddenly sank in the river bed.

Was it in Hwangji or Sabook?
A naked child played alone in the yard
where muck was heaped like an old tomb.

What hunger did he suffer from?
In the yard he pressed mud together to build a house,
fondling his baby penis.
Sometimes an ant climbed onto the back of his hand,
and red salvia bloomed gently by the muck heap.

Why was the mother who went out to fetch white clouds not returning?
Only the lips of salvia pushed open the bush clover door of the mud house to enter.

Suicide of the Mother Tree 2

What did I see that day, chewing on my mother's flesh?

Trāyastrimśa,* a huge pupil in the thirty-third heaven, opened wide, inwardly, and all at once the capillaries grasping it began to dry up. What did I see that day—a large birch turned to coal, Bari abandoned and set afloat on the sea, or a daughter returning from travels in the other world to save her father who had deserted her? I cautiously chewed the sad leaf of transfiguration—nasty transfiguration. The old dark leaf of a dry tongue had shriveled up, not slick like a newborn baby, and ground its own body with the sound of whetting, *seogreak seogreak*.

Yes, also the pupil. Though I wanted to defenestrate the sky and place a warm piece of flesh on your spoon, Bari, my mother, death flew by in pairs. Wasn't the bright white milk of her exhausted body the miracle cure she brought after wandering in the underworld? Bari, wasn't it her nettle-like body of a winter tree that gave her swollen breasts to her father, and then fell into a sound sleep, dead tired? The death named life was far worse. Father, who took to bed again and again with deadly diseases for his sin, please die for me. The night was coming when red spots of fever would break out on the birch tree, bare as the moon, and pour down petals, bloody discharges, the last petals like river water.

Baby, give me bells and a knife.
On the night when the leaves shook madly and bells rang, what knife stuck in someone's pupil was the desiccated tongue I chewed and swallowed?

*Trāyastrimśa, the thirty-third heaven, is the name of the second heaven in Buddhist cosmology (Translators' note).

The Other Side of a Caress

When I take off my shirt and eat a watermelon,
the fly resting on my toe
burrows into my breast.
Even waving my hand is tiring, so I give it a fierce stare.

Whoops, maybe it's evidence of rot.

Did it sense that I no longer believe anyone?
A few digestive pills are all I can offer to my crooked toe,
to the hope that has suffered so many boils on my toe.
Is it apparent that I have come to say
"Yes," in a non-humiliating way?

The agony of my soul stinking
within my tough, safe belly.
(Why is only the exposed anus ugly?)

I say "I love you madly"
instead of "I like to sleep with you."

Are his innards also rotting?
I feel dizzy. Those bewitched germs
reproducing wildly in my climax!

Pasque Flower

Because she's really short and doesn't covet sunlight, she hears the sigh of the wind roaming under her ankles.

When people come across her by a grave, of all places, they speak of her graceful figure. Some read into her the sorrow of living in a remote place. Then she giggles, hunching her shoulders and shaking the slanting tresses of her hair.

She doesn't shed her petals to keep a promise. She despises flowers falling feebly as tears. The slanted shake of her head, with its age spots and disheveled hair, may hold your ankles. Perhaps you harbor the odor of your own skeleton.

From the moment of her birth she wanted to grow old. So she disdained her roots, which can break even rocks, in order to grow. One day she may say to you, "Hey, look? This is all!" The pasque flower bloomed between you and me.

Airborne Was the Airplane

When for the first time I boarded the plane to Kangneung,
my wings, wishing to become sound,
bounced 6000 feet up into the sky.
As a cloud is carried on itself,
I hoped that if I fell from the plane, before touching ground,
my flesh would dissolve into vapor,
and my dry bones would fall into the silver aspen forest
of Daekwan-ryeong, where hope might grow upward and out.
My shin and breastbones and skull would flutter
one after another in greenest harmony.
Airborne was the airplane; the tar-like village
of humanity was far below,
but, ah, the sky was warm.
I was traveling there at a speed of 800 or 900 kilometers per hour
to pick flowers for my withered mother.
Mountain cherries burning — *snap, crackle* — green embers in their fading
were in full bloom on the spring mountain.

The Dwelling Place of Love

Don't speak. Don't say anything. This tree is growing here like this because it also has a thought.
         — Chuang Tzu

They say life is like that
and that a time will come even to love disease.

When I come across a face
that carries a sadness hard to cure,

a beggar woman with a long neck —
I'm free, I'm a complete ruin,
nothing to do with all the things you want,

her eyes gaze at me in silence —
I feel like I have become an empty house.

They say life is like that,
and I feel like my spirit is living in another body.
A time will come to love even that.

I Lie Down on the Cloud Pillar

In search of Euryale ferox*, I go to Cloud Pillar Temple†, which has never bloomed with Euryale ferox. Wretched Buddha heads greet me. I am twenty-nine today.

Though some 247,000 hours have passed through me, my hours have not reached the old star yet. My heart often plays a trick on my knees — horrendous days on which my knees suffer no injury, though I fall down, pass without a dirge.

Mounting the cloud pillar — the higher I climb, the deeper the valley grows — I see the lying Buddhas. I am nineteen today.

The chisels and hammer of the stonemason, who ascended hastily to heaven when a rooster crowed at the wrong time, were reduced to dust. This southern land, where a man and a woman lie like Buddhas, unable to sit up, swells with spring waters surging in the East Sea.

It is very warm, they will sink into the water, soon their blood will circulate.

I whisper *Talitha cumi*˙, *Talitha cumi* into the ears of the Buddha who cannot walk. Though someone says in my ear over and over again, "Girl, arise, arise."

I lie down on the cloud pillar, as in the nap into which I fell inside the wardrobe where I had hidden while waiting for my mother: I am nine today.

Passing through the afternoon dream, the night dream, and the dawn dream, I grow small as a pinkie. I lie in the larger sea and watch: from a bulb buried somewhere in my mother's body, in the depths of the East Sea, a flower stalk, raw flesh, a blood clot and bundle of flowers, tears the flesh of water and soars, and the sun rises.

I lie down and cry among the swaying leper Buddhas stuck in the wide sea like thorns. No, I cannot cry because I have been sleeping since I was born and could not see the Euryale ferox emerging from its flower at the end.

The House Is Cold

A whale died in my dream last night.
Sailors are said to exclaim that red flowers
are opening when they see blood
spurting from a harpooned whale just before it dies.
Someone was much too desolate
to dare look at the blooms.

I collect the petals and build paper lanterns
to hang from the ceiling and windows.
Perhaps this old house might have thought
of committing suicide for a long time.
It seemed to take its thirsty veins
out of its body on rainy nights.

I set the paper lantern on the crest of a wave.
I heard there is a shore on this planet
where whales return to die.
Why do they have to go to sea
knowing they cannot shake off the memory of lungs and womb?

Two whales are dead; a dead baby calf was found
in the womb of a large whale who roamed for a long time
in my dream last night, stuck with harpoons.
Through a chink in the door, its blood-red flowers
flew out, soaking the playground and tree-lined street.
The shore is far away,
the dead house is already cold.

Coarse Sand

I come to the spring sea at Jeongdong, Kangneung
to enjoy the moon
with my mother, who has long suffered from a chronic disease.

In a handful of sand the spring days go *shwaa*,
and in a handful of sand the eyes of seven children ripen.

"Aren't they beautiful?"
she says, handing me a few grains of coarse sand.
They say that if you do something unusual death is near:
my heart sinks when she says,
like a girl clicking her false teeth,
"Aren't they beautiful?"

Does sand remember pebbles?
Do pebbles miss the time when they were rocks?

Night travels deep into the spring sea,
my mother has winnowed *shwaa* her whole life.

The bone of something that cried as its ribs wore down
lies on its back in the palm of my hand.

On a ridge in Daekwan-ryeong
a rock house, which is splitting inside, places the moon on its head.

Dried Pollack Soup

I saw a man in the street.
He looked familiar,
my thousand-year-old heart glowed.
The cold river, which could not be crossed, was deep;
only a petal fluttered down.

If we go amiss in this life, what wind of a valley will we become?
I lay the drunken man down on the warm floor
and beat the dried pollack;
shamefully, I shed my skin to pick out the thin flesh
and cooked a bowl of hot soup for him.

When I awoke after a sound
fermented sleep of a thousand years,
I found myself gone;
only my bones were piled
neatly on the dining table.

Something invisible
slops in the shining empty bowl.

Kobau's Salted Grill House

How strange it is! When pork is grilled over the briquette fire in the Kobau House in Sinchon, when ragged faces eat the salted meat with relish, rubbing the grill with thick chunks of fat,

the flesh that secretly moved inside the sacrum or ribcage bound to muscle on the other side of the body, of those who were unable to touch each other's flesh in life — strange indeed —

the lump of executed desire that must have licked the back of its young and gone into heat rubs its flesh with its own flesh, smelling a friendly scent as if to say, I miss you and so forth.

Under the bare electric bulb, a few women with glowing faces are butchering a pig on a big cutting board, as if my flesh is rubbing my own flesh they cheerfully cut the raw meat,

while I, like a dancing girl at a festival, wrap bells, dagger, and a few pieces of meat in a leaf of lettuce and swallow it, how strange! life suddenly becomes simple and light and clear, and all of sudden my face, which I have never seen, appears.

A Sea Eel's Yawn

When I saw a sea eel filleted in a raw fish restaurant, its head cut off and skin peeled away, it fluttered and pricked its head with its whole body, which had become a thorn of white sorrow, and when I saw its head give up the last yawn of its life, gently opening its mouth wide, almost solitarily, then closing it forever, I grew a little sad that life had become so desolate.

When I saw by the seashore in Nokdong near Sorok Island a basket of sea eels auctioned off and skinned, and forty heads opening their mouths wide and then slowly taking their last breath, I don't know why, but there was no place for sadness or loneliness to break in, and, strangely, something like a quiet annihilation spread into my mind as emptiness.

I thought something unexpected had caused them to return as in the past, and absent-mindedly watched the women's casual cutting and the eels' long, quiet yawns. It all seemed perfectly peaceful, despite the discharge of the fishy, sweetish odor.

When I raised my eyes, I could see the island of white deer and lepers, and little by little a deep blue horn grew from my head, and my knuckles decayed in exactly the same ratio.

Afternoon Lady

Because the word *Sabha** was so pretty,
she wanted to live in the Sabha world.
Because the word Sabha was so pretty,
the woman pricked my heart with her nail.
She had white, pink, and yellow nails
and her black pupil ripened,
stealthily peeking into my heart.
With so many nails,
the flowers would soon open.
It was four o'clock† when the scars of the nails deepened.

*In Buddhism, *Sabha* is the world of suffering in which we live, in contrast to paradise, or the Land of Happiness (Translators' note).
†Another name for an afternoon lady (*mirabilis jalapa*), which is also called the Marvel-of-Peru (Translators' note).

The Road to Dosol Hermit

How strange! This road bends
wherever you look at it.

My body also bends with the road:
with two legs, then four limbs,
and then my whole body, I lay myself down on the road.

Beautiful fish scale: a swift animal
disappearing into the woods, hemming my waist.

Was it a dream,
my sorrow used to stand up straight?

My forty-something sister, who married at twenty-nine,
flashes across my whole body
to begin a winter retreat.

Narrow Gate

In the mourner's house, people are busily coming and going and soup is boiling in the corner. They are collecting condolence money, or playing flower cards in twos and threes. There are some familiar faces. My friends are turning gray. Alas, I died at the age of forty-three.

My face in the open casket is sallow, and light purple hydrangeas bloom in the yard. What I remember from life — that this flower is suited to death — suddenly makes me sad.

I have not decayed for ten days. People are waiting. They cannot close the casket and carry it to the burial site until I begin to rot: evidence that my soul is finally free. Unfortunately, when they cannot see this sign, word of my deeds in life begins to spread.

A pale man enters. Taking advantage of the commotion, he puts maggots on my face and behind my back. Some notice what he is doing but pretend not to see, because there are too many bodies not rotting.

The maggots crawl into my eyes and nose. I'm about to sneeze but restrain myself, because his hands are trembling. "Finally it begins to rot!" someone changing incense shouts. People hastily close the lid of the casket. Finally I walk through the narrow gate.

I don't know whether the man who helped me across the threshold loved me or not. Trailing my heavy body to lay myself down in the newly dug red grave, I see the shadow of hydrangeas from the old days swaying over my brow, like a pendulum.

Morning Glory

A crossroads.

A male bee starts down the road.
He opens a door to enter, but doesn't come out.

Let's wait.

Once I also came out
through that door.

Asking the Flower Garden for Directions

1.

Last night a baby was placed on my table. Its face was like a tiny yellow pill. Hearing the merry sounds of anxiety with a cold sadness, I slowly put on my surgical gloves.

2.

It was last spring when the baby knocked on the door to my operating room.

I was on my way to Taebaek. Royal azaleas bloomed in abundance. The flowers sent me a message to come get a transfusion, so I went to rid myself of dirty blood. From the dining car of the train I saw, vacantly, how the wind makes a cliff in the air. It was when the train passed Sabok that a slate-grey roof appeared at the end of the road, where an abandoned mine tottered like a woman with bound feet and dropped into a valley. Was it a mountain cherry? A girl on the bench under the shadow of a desolate flower was staring at the railroad, looking for the train, absently clutching her knees and combing the long tresses of her hair.

On my way to Taebaek yellow, sticky mucus dropped from the rim of a dish like an old pistil. The inflamed eyes of a young animal that has known loneliness and fear suddenly crouched inside the royal red azalea petals at the Cheonjedan*. Don't come to me, don't, I shouted, breaking the stalks of the flowers.

3.

It was this summer when I met the baby again.

After the flood, thin and shabby things were swept away or toppled while the wealthy castle grew stronger. Because poor fathers couldn't cast off the disease of hope, the sound of their shoveling didn't stop and flowed into the flooding stream as broken glass beads. I saw the boy at the end of summer. At the end of a wall, where bedcovers were hung, their red peony patterns blazing, the child stood blankly under a crack, clutching a piece of broken brick. A rusted bicycle wheel and an empty Ramen box lay like stray goats. Sunlight caught in the spokes and clinked, the boy seemed to hear nothing. Some passengers were passing around bottles of soju, but he didn't look at them. He stood there blankly, clutching the broken brick.

Then the shadow of the boy's eye swayed. I knew at once it was the face of the girl I saw while passing through Sabok. Boy, won't you come see the sunflowers? Quietly I offered him my hand. If you want, you can come to my operating room.

4.

A gray rat climbs the long sunflower stalk.
Fog flows into the sad womb of a sunflower
whose seeds are devoured, the blood of the warm moon is milky.

On a night of dense fog, the boy came to me through the sunflower whose seeds were devoured. I could smell the blood of the moon in his long hair.

I carried the boy holding the broken brick and laid him on the operating table. Soon he fell asleep on my ribs, twisting his neck to the left like an alpine plant. With the scalpel I carefully cut into his chest, where the shadow of a flower tossed and turned.

5.

My baby is all right. The operation went perfectly. When I cut open the petals
of a mountain cherry, royal azaleas bloomed, and when I cut open the pistils of a
royal azalea, red peonies bloomed. The blood of the warm milky moon flowed
into the boy's heart, as I cut sunflowers and threw them onto the cruel current.
The shining yellow gun barrel sucked in the current and shot off seeds like fire-
crackers. Outside the window, a trumpet vine, which is said to bloom, despising
summer heat, dropped a bucket into its own flower stalk and asked for directions.
It was a night when the moon red as a seal rose cool and hot behind the sun.

*An altar to make sacrifices to Heaven, located on the summit of Taebaek Moun-
tain (Translators' note).

Icicle

Let's pray for what flows.
(That condensed desire!)

I flow into you
and our steps, as if promised, turn bright.
Drops of water keep bouncing.
Now let's just stand upside down.

What flows,
what flows down into you,
only if it can flow along the ridges of my body
and become rapids in a deep gorge,
only if it can wash off the extravagant blood.
(That transparent interior of desire!)

Now let's stop for the time being:
A flame burns in the gap of this stopping.
I will flow into you, losing myself.
(Spring — flower bundle of that knife blade — saturate!)

White Magnolia Flowers Fall

Strange is the snowstorm coming across the valley.
Where did I meet this host of snow flowers?
If you were a snowstorm before you came to me
as a flower, who was I?
On a clear spring day
the lower part of the abdomen suddenly grew cold
and in the valley placed alongside the entrails
lies the shrine of Shakyamuni Buddha's sarira,* which opened up without flowers or leaves.

Ice melts and haze flows,
but why are you swaying with such a chilly smile?
Everywhere you laugh cracks a little,
and the root of the valley tingles.

They say poison is killed by poison—
was it the poison of intense desire that melted the frozen earth?
The dream of a snowstorm runs backward.

Every April morning
I feared magnolia flowers would fall.
Snowstorm, you prepared the way for a suicide
under the twilight crashing and spreading into its own flesh.
Like the cotton coils fluttering in the backyard,
you dressed up at dawn.

What were you before you came to me as a flower?
A waterfall standing upside down or a brass ring writhing in the mud?
Because my poison is still the hot hope of my groin
I cannot see the bare face of despair, which comes
to kill despair. I cannot grasp your ankle.

* Buddhist term for bodily relics of spiritual masters (Translators' note).

Time Lasts Long

In this valley
are buried the falling stars of my lost love.
What I feel when I reach up to touch the leaves
must be green mixed with red.

How many loves my fingers have touched
in order to learn how to tell colors
without opening my eyes?

How shyly the age of my first period visited me
like the passionate loves of twenty, twenty-one, and twenty-five,
when I wished to grow old quickly!
Our flag is not too far away
to be swallowed up as a beautiful scar.

Now in this valley of changing autumn colors
please don't say nostalgia in haste.
Only after serving the shadow of time with their whole bodies
do birches return to the winter mountain.
You should talk about birches only through birches.

Falling stars, palms with red-hot brands.
When pretty white bones are gathered again
in the case of remains deep in your heart,
please come to the autumn mountain at the hour
when the afternoon shadow combs the sunlight of noon.

Sunwoo Kim was born in 1970 and studied Korean literature in college. She has published five books of poetry: *If My Tongue Refuses to Remain in My Mouth* (2000), *Falling Asleep under Peach Flowers* (2003), *Who Is Sleeping in My Body?* (2007), *To My Endless Revolution* (2012), and *A Nocturne* (2016); several books of nonfiction; and four novels: *I Am a Dance* (2008), *Candle Flower* (2010), *Lovers of Water* (2012), and *A Prayer: Yoseok and Wonhyo* (2015). She has received the Modern Literary Award and the Cheon Sangbyung Poetry Award.

Won-Chung Kim is a professor of English Literature at Sungkyunkwan University in Seoul, Korea, where he teaches contemporary American poetry, ecological literature, and translation. He earned his Ph.D. in English at the University of Iowa in 1993. He has translated ten books of Korean poetry, including Chiha Kim's *Heart's Agony*, Hyonjong Chong's *The Dream of Things*, and *Cracking the Shell: Three Korean Ecopoets*. He has also translated E.T. Seton's *The Gospel of the Redman* and H.D. Thoreau's *Natural History Essays* into Korean. His first book of poetry, *I Thought It Was a Door*, was publihed in 2014.

Christopher Merrill has published six collections of poetry, including *Boat* and *Watch Fire*, for which he received the Lavan Younger Poets Award from the Academy of American Poets; several edited volumes, among them, *The Forgotten Language: Contemporary Poets and Nature* and *Flash Fiction International: Very Short Stories from Around the World*; and six books of nonfiction, most recently, *The Tree of the Doves: Ceremony, Expedition, War* and *Self-Portrait with Dogwood*. He directs the University of Iowa's International Writing Program.